December ... 79

To Robert :

*May this streetlamp
help light your way....*

Thank you, and good luck!

Laeret N. Horovitz

STREETLAMP, TREETOP, STAR

STREETLAMP, TREETOP, STAR

by

David D. Horowitz

Rose Alley Press
Seattle, Washington

For information, please contact the publisher:

Rose Alley Press
4203 Brooklyn Avenue NE, #103A
Seattle, WA 98105-5911
telephone: 206-633-2725
e-mail: rosealleypress@juno.com

The author gratefully acknowledges that the following poems in this book first appeared or will soon appear in other publications:

Art Word Quarterly: Near Distance; Night Vision
Candelabrum: Tree Ring; To a Working Poet; Sage; Conjunction
The Lyric: The True Mean; Reminder
Pegasus: Stars and Lamps (poem accepted for publication, printed in this book with editor's permission)
Phase and Cycle: Leafy Knoll; The Humanities; Relevant (Lunchtime Concert: Vivaldi's Music) (original title: Relevant (On a Lunchtime Concert of Vivaldi's Music)); Dusk Horizon
Plains Poetry Journal: Iron Madonna, 1989
Rashi: To a Jewish Woman Praying in a Synagogue
The Red Candle Treasury: *An Anthology of Poems from the Period 1948-1998*, M.L. McCarthy, ed., The Red Candle Press, 1998: Tree Ring
Riverrun: Credit; Go, Seek; Two Poems for a Police Officer Who Committed Suicide After Being Harassed for a Decade by His Peers; The Victorious; 1994
Tucumcari Literary Review: Chapter 7; Aviary (original title: Some Notes on Birds); Note to a Cynic; America; True Community; The Classics; Resource (To a Unitarian Church); Mentor; Café Authentic; City Fog; Metamorphosis; Song; Evening Embrace; Stars; Too; In Praise of Evening Air

Library of Congress Catalog Card Number: 99-70283

ISBN: 0-9651210-5-4

With the artist's gracious permission, this book's cover features a reproduced image of "Night Geometry" by Paul Havas, 1986.

Printed in the United States of America

ACKNOWLEDGMENTS

I want to thank the following people for helping me mature as a writer and, or produce this book: William Dunlop, for valuable initial guidance; Victoria Ford and Michael Spence, for their comments about this manuscript; Paul Havas, for allowing me to use a reproduced image of one of his paintings as the basis for this book's cover; my mother, Ruth L. Horowitz, for her support and encouragement; and my late grandfather, Louis Horowitz, for his generosity. Many other people have helped and encouraged me over the years. Let me now simply say to them: thank you.

I would like to add two observations. First, while many poets, including myself, write about personal experience, poetry itself is not simply autobiography. Unless otherwise noted, poems in this book are not about particular people; indeed, names used in them are either fictitious or those of famous historical figures. Second, I assume full responsibility for the views expressed in this book. The aforementioned people helped me develop aesthetically and, or produce this book; they are not responsible for my views.

CONTENTS

STREETLAMP, TREETOP, STAR

CLOUDS

We drift beneath the heavens, graze

      The mountain peaks, and haze

            Horizon pearl-peach and gray.

                  We dissipate in storms, and flood

The valleys, green the hillsides, bud

      The spring, spectrum evenings, mud

            The fertile fields, freshen towns, and mist

Until...   we do not exist?

RESULTS

Just after twilight...hillsides black as char
  Against maroon-black peaks
  Below chill opal streaks
And a beauty mark of star.

Gulls slice and circle, romping in the breeze
  Above a heartsick soul
  Whose evening harbor stroll
The beauty cannot quite appease.

How much injustice should restraint endure?
  Avenge the slight?...No,
  In excellence's slow
Persistence she feels sure,

Not violence's quick results.
More stars emerge, raise vision, calming pulse.

SAGE

You master a craft,
Love a few friends,
And ignore pettiness.
Amazingly, you laugh
Despite despair; you never joke
About cruelty, just the vanity of tyrants.
Bitter but polite, your words
Cleanse even the sharpest wounds.

MENTOR

His yearning:
To reach
Beyond the known

And, having grown,
Begin to teach,
Still learning.

EVENING EMBRACE

The afterglow of crimson sun
　　Illuminates the jasmine sky
Where haze and cloud and light are one
　　And seagulls circulate their cry.

The mountains silhouette the scene
　　As, in the foreground, traffic glides
Past darkness-blackened evergreens
　　And neighborhoods where noise subsides.

I sip the scene's serenity
　　And feel the earth and sky embrace,
And from this park, this little space,
　　My heart can reach eternity.

SILHOUETTED

Horizon dims. A single cloud
    Levitates above silhouetted peaks.
        Salmon, pearl, and blue, the sky no longer burns,

Providing ponds of patience, holy space
    For souls reaching past
        Some branchy web of circumstance
            That needs be battled through, straining

Benevolence. The quiet, distant beauty
    Absorbs and mollifies. The city below
        Blossoms light, pulses pleasure.

The generous do not begrudge a nighttime strut,
    But they admire virtue's trek
        Along an isolated ridge.
The peaks begin to blur. Horizon darkens.

STILL LIFE

Rats. Rotten rations. Big guards' random clouts.
A pocky wall, bulb-exposed. A mat.
Wept out, hopes dry to doubts.
No mail. No phone. No this, no that.
So why go on?
Life, even this, within penumbral hell
Is more than when it's gone.
Life, still life, in a barren cell.

A rat...there....No, there it goes....

Liberty.

THE VICTORIOUS

You struggled, fought, and died for liberty,
And still your tyrant keeps his tyranny.
Yet, though his face still rules the public square
And soldiers hose away the bloodstains there,
They've seeped beyond his walls. We know you died,
No matter how the tyrant tries to hide
Your tank-crushed corpses, burnt to smoke and ash,
Incinerated like the daily trash.
We know his words are smoke. He cannot hide
The worth of liberty, for which you died.

FOR A TIBETAN BUDDHIST MONK,
IMPRISONED FOR THIRTY-THREE YEARS
FOR A SINGLE EXPRESSION OF DISSENT

Electric cattle prods searing your teeth
    And handcuffs gouging your wrists,
    Your heart and soul resist
The guards' demands, *their* death,
    Not yours, achieved by fists
That torture flesh like it was meat.

THE CLASSICS

I

The textbook classic you enjoyed last year—
Its cover showing fountains, parks, and deer—
Was written by a man of peace
Murdered by the czar's police.

II

"What a handsome face," the student sighed
Of the poet who could make her sad,
Quite unaware of how the poet died:
In prison for his verses, starving, mad.

CREDIT

The golden lights of commerce trim the bay
As isolated tugs and ferries
Traffic in transition to the night.
Beyond the touch of human hands
Apricot cream mist
Above the silhouetted range
Comforts, as a planet beacons
Hope and perseverance
To those committed to restraint
When rage is all they feel.
The beauty relaxes them
To resilient gratitude,
To commitment no one credits,
For no one could witness the violence
Such commitment helped prevent.

PASSIONATE RESTRAINT

Such hatred seethes within my heart,
Its core becomes a silver dart;
Such hatred seethes within my marrow,
It shapes each bone into an arrow;
Such hatred seethes within my mind
It now can maim and stab and blind....
Yet I restrain my violence, and must,
Or gaining vengeance, lose all trust,
And losing trust, destroy my heart
And marrow, mind and soul, and art.

LEAFY KNOLL

I pray for personal and public peace,
    For though this sounds like mere cliché,
Deep prayer provides resilience and release
    From hatred that can sear away

All cooling patience in a person's soul,
    And leave one prone to fight and feud
That finally consumes all self-control.
    Across a wilderness of mood

Each individual must venture, soul
    Retested by each obstacle.
Just now, I rest beside prayer's leafy knoll.
    My heart stays warm, my temper cool.

STREET SMART

I woke this morning, full of rage,
    So bitter I could barely speak.
I poured my anger on a page
    And only then felt some relief.

I walked outside for sun and air
    And swam jade light beneath a tree,
Distracting me from my despair,
    Recalling some serenity.

I strolled the tree-lined streets, and saw
    That life continued as before.
A neighbor's greeting helped me thaw
    And feel some warmth within my core.

The rage within my heart still beats,
    The pain I felt still feels like pain,
But I remembered on those streets
    A simple stroll can keep one sane.

THE HUMANITIES

The silence of the stars excites
    Imagination to believe
It hears divinity in distant lights
    Hum harmonies of warming love

That help the lonely persevere,
    That help the pained endure.
Let supernovas blast! The stars appear
    Serene, and so console and cure.

Let science honestly explore,
    Report the truth of what it sees;
But let the poetry within our core
    Explore and reach—or freeze.

TO A JEWISH WOMAN
PRAYING IN A SYNAGOGUE

You pray in thoughtful silence. Rich and deep
Emotions rise within your soul. The prayers
Release a hymn of hope within your heart, asleep
To Jewish sentiments for many years.
You own no *kippah*, *tallit*, or *siddur*.
You know no Hebrew, yet you hear through walls
Of centuries appeals to God from sore
And noble spirits. Desperate Hebrew calls
Resound and resonate within your core.
You fill with warmth and pride, not knowing why
Your soul identifies with Hebrew, or
How songs you never heard could make you cry.

GO, SEEK

You needn't stuff your soul into a little case,
Presentable to some authority,
But stiffening and suffocating you.

The dogmatist erases every trace
Within his soul of thoughtful liberty,
Of love of anything complexly true.

What doesn't fit his theories cannot be
Endured, nor can the freedom to pursue,
Explore, and doubt. Go, seek more mental space;

Roam amongst ideas. Consider any view
Which might lead you to truth. Such liberty
No person should deny, or could replace.

TO A WORKING POET

You numb yourself to finish tasks, strain
    Against routine, and squeeze some meaning
    From jobs you find demeaning,
Deriving purpose from your pain.

At night you write. Your marrow bleeds truths.
    Your soul rejoices in this effort,
    And, for a second, joins forever
A feeling with a phrase, and so renews.

COURTLY
(COMPOSED AFTER READING
SEVERAL LITERARY BIOGRAPHIES)

My first reaction was dismay, disgust—
The grinning gossip, rivalries, and schemes,
Hypocrisy so skilled it made distrust
The only rational response, and "seems"
A strong assertion of validity.
The pompous lords! Pretentious ladies! Vain
And vicious frauds who bred aridity
When self-absorbed, and decimating pain
When slightly angry or perturbed! Oh,
I had….I still admire poetry
From those momentous eras. But, no,
I'll not again presume that history
Then equalled greatest art. Fond hope,
And yet there were some noble lords, and, yes,
Great Shakespeare, Jonson, Dryden, Swift, and Pope,
In spite of faults, endured and won success,
And merit highest praise, for even then
The greats were hounded by the lowest men.

SUCH DEPTH AND VIRTUE

To say one thing and mean another,
And smile, then betray your brother;
To value power more than truth,
And thus turn model for our youth;
To worship money, sex, and praise,
And help the poor because it pays;
To deem duplicity a need
When fighting phoniness and greed;
To spy and steal, yet seem to stoop,
So as to rise within a group;
To hound the man who lives alone
And read his mail and tap his phone;
To harass strangers on command
And think such action plain and bland;
To teach indifference to the laws
So long as crime is for a cause—

Such depth and virtue now pervade;
Mere liberty and justice fade.

I

I drowned my anger in a river.
No one heard or cared
How deeply I despaired.
They urged, "Be a giver."

They spied and wiretapped, harassed.
No one heard or cared
How deeply I despaired.
They urged, "Explore your past."

They grinned and cooed, "We pity you."
No one heard or cared
How deeply I despaired.
They urged, "Remember, you're a Jew!"

They watched, controlled my calls and mail.
No one heard or cared
How deeply I despaired.
They urged, "You cannot fail."

They drove me from a job, but I withstood.
No one heard or cared
How deeply I despaired.
They urged, "It's for your good."

They preached at me Community and Charity.
No one heard or cared
How deeply I despaired.
They urged, "Think parity."

They craved success, through "love" they claimed.
No one heard or cared
How deeply I despaired.
They urged, "The Right's (or Left's) to blame!"

I raised my anger from the river.
No one heard or cared
How deeply I despaired.
They urged, "Be a forgiver."

I kept my anger dry, and learned
To listen to my rage
And write it on a page
And, with that rage, return.

DISTANT AWARENESS
(A UNITED STATES MEDITATION)

The headlines holler distant danger
Of murder, torture, bombing, war
Exploding from the kind of anger
That frequently flares here

Where peace and plenty, love and leisure
Grace millions. Often I myself
Have raged to hurt, to murder,
Restrained by law, and love, and wealth.

AMERICA

Corruption, friend, flows from the top,
  And those there now were once abused.
They'll want revenge before they stop,
  And they might kill who might accuse.

The blackmailed pro they can control;
  Integrity like yours they fear.
Expect to be harassed your whole
  Life—but stay sincere: persevere!

1994

Your every action's watched and known.
   Your every spoken word is heard.
A spy is there when you're alone
   Recording when your burp occurred.

Retreating to a private self,
   In silence now alone you trust.
The camera sees you through its stealth
   But cannot sense your real disgust

For power's new intrusive toys
   Recording all you say and do,
Delimiting and tainting joys,
   And blind to understanding you.

TRUSTED ADVISOR

What bribery and blackmail can suppress
And calculating underlings confess
Can save our champion from scandal.
Some shrewd publicity can handle
What silence we can't buy. Mistrust
Can be manipulated into guess.
Deny all charges: feign disgust,
And glow as simply as a candle.

Remember: they'd do the same to us.

TWO POEMS
FOR A POLICE OFFICER WHO COMMITTED SUICIDE
AFTER BEING HARASSED FOR A DECADE BY HIS PEERS

I

Ten years ago your partner beat
A handcuffed prisoner, so you
Reported it. Back on the street
You walked your beat alone—pariah. True
To principle (your partner cleared),
Your steady work excelled
As "snitch," "rat," and worse were smeared
Across your locker door; compelled
To act on principle, but hurt,
Your hell stayed hidden ten full years
Before you blasted bullets through your heart
And earned, at funeral, the praise of peers.

II

Tormentors sense a weakness. Yours
Was wanting their approval. Ostracized
For principle and honesty, harassed
By bullies seeking sport, at last
You fired back—your suicide
Completed their campaign. You locked the doors
And opened up your heart. Two shots.
Your uniform, though bloody, kept its crease.
Your heart, which had been tied in knots,
Perhaps found some release.

DUSK HORIZON

Lilac-ruby swathes horizon
Echoing daytime heat.
A gull circle-searches in-
To receding silent solitude.
Dusk drops darkness
Onto the laps of lawns
And into the filling tree-baskets,
And then prepares for sleep itself.
First, it salves the wounded,
Consoles the sore and weary,
Revives the lonely to seek
Companionship in nighttime faces
Or work to truths alone
That light some hope till morning.

CIRRUS TWILIGHT

Saffron cirrus crisp the atmosphere
As cyan chills to darkness. Contrails
Fluff, disintegrate, and disappear
As horizon pales.

Soon twilight blackens. Stars
And streetlamps reveal their brilliance.
The nighttime seeps, and stirs
Resignation—to resilience.

THE ONLY CURE

Betrayed, your heart can never heal
Without the medicine of honesty
Applied with salve of tact, to help it feel
Love's trust again, truth's remedy.

Yes, honesty can heal, not hurt,
As you, deprived of it by all,
So eloquently could assert,
So sick of your mistrust, your trusted wall.

CAFÉ AUTHENTIC

Their pastries hum honey, not shout sugar;
Their floor glows maple, not linoleum;
A band—guitar and fiddle and aching tenor—
Relax the center of the window-fronted room,
So, when you enter,
The blend of dialogue and tune
So warms your blood
You feel like honey spread
On fresh banana bread,
Sweet but not sugary.

EACH

Just look: those cookies! wheel-sized oatmeal raisin,
Honey-cashew, gingerbread, three kinds of chocolate chip!
Just look: that muffin bursting
With apples, currants, walnuts, spice;
Or pumpkin or zucchini or banana bread—
A hefty, heavy slice
With herbal tea or fresh, thick juice to sip
On evening's patio, horizon honey-saffron red....

Behind me, flyers smother corkboard wall—full
Of poetry and times, t'ai chi classes, acting seminars,
Guitars and flutes and violins for sale,
And rooms for rent. I contemplate
Day's tumble of events, and nibble cookie, sip
Pineapple juice. The great
Stay humble, yet reach for stars,
Attend to how they bake each chocolate chip.

CHAPTER 7

FOR LEASE Call Tim at ...-7658
Inside the still-stained carpet catches dust.
All else is gone, but resonating space.
Above, on eaves, I notice rust.

Ten years ago, Bob still did busy trade.
Students tracked down deals in here, found texts,
Classics, for quarters. Reading fiends would raid
The plywood shelves; and browsers test

For bargains, often buy; and faculty
Would even sniff around, and mull, decide
They could for their research buy two or three,
And thus help Bookin' Bob....That declined,

Declined until this tomb of store remains
Collecting dust. What's next? A health food shop,
Or restaurant? A video arcade?
Computer goods? Some student stop

For coffee, conversation, and croissants?
Some fast food franchise? Vintage clothes? Who knows....
I note the barrenness, what ambiance
Endures...and walk to *Rose and Rows*

And buy two books of poetry, and one of prose.

THAT'S ENTERTAINMENT! II

No soundtrack, just horizon pink
As conch, and peach as nectar;
The skyline-glistening business sector
Shimmers....Lights atop a TV-tower blink
And traffic echoes rosy haze
Reposing, Venus ablaze
Beside the moon. No actor,
Bomb, or chase scene. Subtle grays,
Though, as I've never seen in films or plays,
Enchanting...prompting me to think.

CANDLEPOWER

Stars silverpoint night sky. Around the lake,
Cars circulate, as on it prinking light,
A gold aurora mixed with red and white
From passing cars, flickers and breaks.

The neon boulevard asserts, as stars
Illumine contemplating hearts, their light
Enchanting instinct. The star-rich night
Frees working minds to leisured longing, stirs

Wonderment and gratitude. The lake,
Fringed with piney lawn, and golden red
With cake candle glow, and overhead
Stars silvershining, quiets hearts awake.

NIGHT BUS

Above a freeway guardrail, lamps
Blaze braille miles, bending
Trails past neighborhoods, up ramps,
Beneath overpasses, descending,
Rising.
      Horizon's maroon hush
Beneath unblinking starlight
Blackens, too. Human galaxies we rush
Through, lamps blanketing night.

STARS

The day has gone to bed. It rests
On saffron pillows in the west.
As our city's streetlamps gleam,
Sky soon will turn off all its lights
Except the stars—to help us dream,
Endure our woes, or reach for heights.

STARS AND LAMPS

The distant silver dots console
And steel resolve to reach its goal.
The constellations speckle sky, as lamps,
Remote, web neighborhoods aglow like camps.
Enduring through the night, they disappear
At dawn; through day their watchers persevere.

CONJUNCTION

Below the cliff and across the bay, lights
Shimmer shoreline; reflections
Gild the inner bay; stars twitter.
Full moon penumbras night.

> Two ferries float on darkness;
> Embrace; kiss

And part serenely.
Atop the cliff, the moon
Grazes a pine branch.

DESIRE

Unused to conversation so direct,
She feels his phrases penetrate her half-
Truths she thought no one could detect,
And feels herself connect
And laugh,
Admitting to herself she'd lied
And for his honesty
Feels gratified,
Feels liberty
Desiring integrity.

TO AN EXCELLENT YOUNG WOMAN

By this point in your life you've heard
   So many beaux and boyfriends swear
Their love for you, another word
   Might simply drive you to despair!

What can I do, though? Denigrate
   Your beauty, talent, warmth, and wit,
Your confidence and strength, your grace,
   Your subtle blend of charm and grit,

Or undermine deserved esteem
   When merit is so evident?
No, talk about you has to mean
   Praise. Briefly, then: you're excellent.

TOO

The heart too hurt to feel, too numb to ache,
Too disappointed now to sympathize
Or feel a thing for someone else's sake
Can, if it feels again, grow truly wise,

Can, if it loves again, first truly love
And heal another's pain. Impatience shouts,
But love can pause and sigh, has seen enough
To know it always faces strains and doubts.

LETTER

I'm strong enough to let you go.
　　You needn't fear harassment, feuds,
　　The threat of suicidal moods
Or violence and stalking—no.
Nor is this meant to prove I'm strong.
　　I want to be considerate—
　　No guilt, no fear, no bitterness,
No last call charm to prove you're wrong,
No correspondence plotted to prolong and show
　　And prove by hashing out our history.
　　I loved you more than you loved me.
That's all we need to know.

ON LIVE MUSIC AT A NEIGHBORHOOD TAVERN

Not only do I *hear* here, but I *see*
The singer grin, the picker pluck and strum,
The drummer tap and pat and hum,
Lighten hearts, and deepen the humanity
Of twenty folks who eat delicious food,
And chat, or, in some lonely corner, brood.

ET TOI!

My marrow yelps as music seeps
  Vitality into my pain. From soil
  Of experience, this zydeco can oil
Stuck hearts and slide them from their sleep.

Accordion and washboard, fiddle, lead
  And bass guitar, and drums awaken sweat
  Of life. Before tonight few here had met:
We drink now, cheer together, dance, and feed.

  This music, of a culture, cries
  Et toi!, and many of us rise.

RELEVANT
(LUNCHTIME CONCERT: VIVALDI'S MUSIC)

This music showers green and sun and song
    Upon these lunchtime listeners
Who feel through harmony that they belong
    Within an ordered universe
Of liberty and love, of right and wrong,
    Where music may still cleanse and nurse
    And help one's mind refresh, one's body hum,
And make one's parts feel like a sum.

TO A BRILLIANT HARPSICHORDIST

I

Such mastery, such musicianship
　　Reflects not merely skill, but soul and joy!
You honor music, playing with the depth
　　Of a man and delight of a boy!

II

You make your harpsichord sound lush
And sparkling.　Your plucked strings can rush,
Then hush, yet resonate; precise
And passionate, their sound delights
Your audience, like lights
From candelabra or sunlight melting ice.

STEEL DRUM BAND

The sunshine cleans the sky of cloud
And coaxes air to warmth and joy.
This music streams and bubbles round
And cleanses minds of misery;
Percussive silver pulses dance
Into the bones of listeners.
Some start to grin and bob and bounce
And cry out. Now some start to dance,
Effusing celebration. Look!
The lead musician starts to grin!

INTO LUSTRE

Commitments narrow and confine
Yet help one focus, then refine
Details, particular details,
Each tiny detail. Craftsmen love
To burnish metal into lustre; or grove
A set of seedlings, tend each twig;
Or twist and polish filigree;
Or locate treasure in a dig,
With brush as well as shovel. Details
Flow from the craftsman's fingers beautifully
Finished.

A GIFT

Patience. T'ai chi gives you patience
To bear injustice
With restraint and principle,
A still, calm center.

Power. T'ai chi gives you power
To build and realize goals
Without undue ambition
Or boasting, a still, calm center.

Prudence. T'ai chi gives you prudence,
Profound intuition
Countering circumstances'
Meanest maneuvers, a still, calm center.

Compassion. T'ai chi gives you compassion,
Sympathy for others' pain
That disciplines your strength,
A still, calm center.

Life. T'ai chi gives you life
Fountaining in marrow and muscle,
Sustaining you through pain
To joys rising through a still, calm center.

NEAR DISTANCE

Clouds moor in flamingo-gold lagoon
   Above beachfront boatmasts, sheds, and palms
   Whose frondy plumage whispers calm
Beneath a full but unobtrusive moon.
Heat sinks into the sand beneath the breeze;
   The spectral skyline's geometric shapes
   Behind the shoreline's still watercraft drape
The bay in reflection and dwarf the trees.
Yet here is an ocean edge, a beach.
   A light on the cusp of distance blinks,
   Exciting those on shore tonight to think
Of all beyond the city's, and humans', reach.

BEAUTY

The valley cradles rosy salmon light
Adjacent bluffs conceal, honey-pearl glowing above them.
Streetlights trace electric grids to the silverback bay....
Serenity cools the city's beauty.
Freeways uncrowd; dinner-scented homes please workers.
Somewhere beyond the night, dusty sun
Smothers a famine-stricken country.
The thought of helping people there
Keeps beauty here.

LINKED
(WRITTEN AFTER ATTENDING AN INTERFAITH CONFERENCE TO DISCUSS THE BOSNIAN CRISIS)

Today within a synagogue
Sat Jews and Moslems, side by side,
Attracted by their faith in God,
Repelled by modern genocide.

The sparkle in the speakers' eyes
Revealed the wound within their hearts.
They spoke of tyrants' boasts and lies,
Of death and scattered body parts,

Of tolerance for different creeds,
Of history and aid and prayer
To sprinkle on the problem, seeds
Which help us grow beyond despair.

That genocide should be the link
To make us share a synagogue
Or mosque or church, should make us think:
What do we know of God?

RESOURCE
(TO A UNITARIAN CHURCH)

The shipwrecked souls who wash ashore
　　In need of love and hope
Sound shell-shocked, as if from a war,
　　And struggle just to cope.

Divorced or bankrupt, friendless, lost,
　　These shipwrecked need a place to rest
Where love does not come at a cost
　　And faith in God is not a test.

They slowly share their pains with us:
　　We sometimes hold a hand.
This helps restore their sense of trust
　　And helps them want to stand.

The pain of life can paralyze
　　The noblest heart and shrewdest mind,
Yet all can learn to recognize
　　How pain can help us grow more kind.

Our church does not promote mere grief
　　As unifying force.
Yet many here provide relief
　　With pain-born wisdom at its source.

COOL WARMTH

Pine hills serrate saffron-gold horizon.
A line of pearl mist divides the hills
From level bay below. In dusk chill,
Horizon's hearth consoles.
Beauty mollifies an observer, pained
But perseverant. Reminded
He can feel gratitude, even warmth,
He recommits himself to love
Carefully parceled out.

IN PRAISE OF EVENING AIR

The mild evening air relaxes me
And helps me turn my pain to patience. Breathe,
And calm the soul; let warmth meet liberty,
And though at home one might despair or seethe,
Out here, along the campus grounds, I stroll
Past autumn leaves—gold, pumpkin, burgundy—
Through life-caressing air, releasing soul
To reach and range, to stretch its sympathy
To all, and feel its place within the whole.

CONSOULED

Beneath pumpkin-pink horizon
Mountains echo autumn's lengthening shadow.
Traffic circulates across the distant bridge
And, headlit now, trickles
Down residential hillside streets above
Navysilver bay. Trafficsound
Washes auburn dusk with cool air.
While chilled trees shed withered flame,
Human beings can release pain, consoled
By buds of wisdom.

REMINDER

Along the blackened bluff last night
  The shore was dotted gold,
Beside the warm horizon light
  And in the evening cold.

I watched the sun descend below
  Horizon's perfect line;
It held a saffron-salmon glow
  That reddened into wine.

Such beauty soothed my bitter heart,
  Reminding me of good,
And helped me want to use my art
  To make it understood.

The world can be so cruel, we curse
  And swear we feel no hope.
A sunset, though, or honest verse
  Can help the bitter cope.

THE PURSUIT OF EXCELLENCE

Meticulous mediocrity schemes against excellence,
Fills boredom with vengeance
And ego with conspiracy.
Articulate liberty learns it threatens
Self-praise addicted to position.
An obedient bully wakes to envelopes of bribes
As a divorcée afraid for her children
Does what she's told and keeps her house.
A poor man inveigles innocence
And finds acceptance in a wealthy gang.
An underling wiretaps his boss's rival's life
And finds the dirt that earns promotion.
Here, glows his supervisor,
Is talent!

GENEROSITY

As power dangles favors,
Approval-seeker wavers
And finally consents to violate
Some laws, and just manipulate
For power's noble cause, which she
Cannot just now articulate,
But which his generosity
Must somehow justify. Bribes fill her purse,
But which is worse?—
No house, or this? And what's a bribe?

TO ONE ONLY BRIEFLY SCANDALIZED

Truth's arrows pierce your lies. Deceit deserves
Exposure, though you now return
To havens of hypocrisy, where others serve
Your wealth and might, and only learn
How better to make you believe
That neither you nor they deceive.

Force, power—these you love, and the nerve
To grab. Already fresh lies patch up old,
And True Believers deem this "bold."

PHILOSOPHER'S PEBBLES

POLI SCI 101

Community can march as *We*
But soon devolve to tyranny
Without a speck of liberty,

Which risks the group, for some may stray,
But better that they go away
Than that they're told and forced to stay.

And, watch, for that community
Respecting private liberty
Evokes the deepest loyalty.

COMMUNITY

We did not *try* to Build Community.
We simply sought the truth so honestly
That mutual respect and unity
Of purpose grew—in short, community.

BROTHERLY LOVE

If I would not earn money to survive,
I'd have to burden someone else, deprive
That person (by degrees) of liberty.

Live freely, brothers! I'll take care of me!

WHOLE WORDS

I
"Consideration," yes, a word of mind
Denoting both the rational and kind.

II
Yes, "thoughtful," too, suggests that mind
And sympathy can be combined.

A PRAYER

Because a hatred long can simmer
And violence quickly flare,
I pray before I eat my dinner
And often try to share.

FIRST

My first concern is not
Should I be Christian or Jew
But, rather, what
Is good, what is true?

CONSISTENCY

At once, I'm sore and numb.
I feel both pain and joy, defeat
And triumph, incomplete
And whole, talkative and dumb,
That life is bittersweet.

NOTE TO A CYNIC

A grape in brine
Cannot yield wine.

NOT JUST TALK

You don't believe in force or fraud, but trade,
So rather than compel, intimidate,
Deceive, demand, insist, manipulate,
Or whine, you quietly persuade.

CLEAR VISION

Wise
Eyes
Sympathize

But not with wise
Lies.

PASSPORT

Travel tests both our ability
To plan, and our flexibility.

NOW

The Land of Was contains my pains and friendships past.
The Future I cannot yet see....
Now offers all that I might be
But won't become unless I live in it at last.

MATURITY AND YOUTH

"Then what identifies men's youth,
   What demarcates those days?"—
A willingness to sacrifice the truth
   For pretty women's praise.

SIZE AND VALUE

Even in stormy seas, a cork may float
As well or better than many a boat.

LOOKING AT LIBERTY

Looking for someone to save you
Will more than likely enslave you.

SWEET AND SOUR

POLITICS

Comrades

They call each other "comrade brother,"
Yet scheme how to betray each other.

Humanitarian's Exception

"We'd all be better red than dead," he said,
Though he feels I'd be better *dead* than read.

To Poet A, Envious of Poet B

Since B emerged upon the scene,
Your face, as well as thought, is green.

IRON MADONNA, 1989

"That painting's neat—those squiggles and those blue
Whatevers. Pollock's influence. I'm not
Sure what it means. I love it, though! It's got...."

"You love it?!"
                    "Yeah, it's something I could do."

TO "MIMIC"

A parrot, I suppose, can imitate
    An eagle, but this does not let it soar.
A mediocrity may mime the great,
    And master mannerisms, nothing more.

NOTES ON THE DEVIL

The Devil thinks that ambiguity
Conceals accountability,
And so he revels in his shades and veils,
In images and masks, as he reveals
Façades and fronts. He has no self within,
Beneath, some *where*. The Devil is mere skin,
A sheath, a face. The Devil is mere style,
But he looks clever—and what a smile!

POWERFUL FEAR

Those who fear public embarrassment
Will often employ private harassment.

URBAN SCENE

Across the bay—the bluff aglitter!
Beneath my feet—the gutter, litter.

SNAPSHOT

So many men have tried to use her
Her eyes now snigger, "Get lost, loser."

INTERESTED

She's interested in showing him
She's not interested in knowing him.

ON MEMORIAL DAY:
FOR AMERICAN SOLDIERS WHO DIED IN BATTLE

For liberty they died, for mine and yours
And yours, who did not have to fight in wars.

SONG

Birdsong flits around the morning, new
    To spring. It hops about the air,
Complementing blossoms, sunlight, dew,
    And joy, and sweetening despair.

AVIARY

The swallow traces impulse on the air;
The robin trills its morning calls;
The brown-capped sparrow hops and flits, and there
The broad-winged seagull guards the tops of walls.
The crow jeers from its lofty perch, and geese
Spear V-like overhead, giving humans peace.

INTO A RIVER

Cucumber, lettuce, sprouts, tomato—salad
Digests. My blood hums scarlet happy river,
Invigorating pallid
Cells, replenishing a healthy liver.

SUPPORTING ROLE

As temp or teacher, waiter, cook,
They plan their lives to practice art,
And in their leisure, write their book,
Perform their concert, act their part,
Fulfill creative talent, and start
Excelling as a teacher, waiter, temp, or cook.

OUR AGE—ONE OPTIMISTIC VIEW

Our age? when men and women both excel
And both can strive, not cower or compel.
Our age? when children from Manila to Milan
Can first see talent, not a shade of tan.
Our age? when Asians yearn with baseball hearts
And Westerners learn martial arts.
Our age? of judgment of ability,
Of open possibility....

JOYFUEL
(FOR OFFICE MANAGERS)

Released from tending to your staff—
    Their questions, crises, pay, insurance—
You see a show, and belly laugh!
    And joyfully restore endurance.

REFUELING

I

Work, but don't grow *too* austere:
Pleasure helps us persevere.

II

Enjoyment helps us labor and toil,
Fills gritty engines with golden oil.

III

Fun!—Delight and danger, risk and joy,
A giddy girl and frisky boy!

IV

Eclectic whimsy frisks and plays,
Flicks golds and greens on sober grays!

TO A BAROQUE COMPOSER

Composing marriage of continuo and flute,
You harmonize and charm, make intimate, not cute.

THE TRUE MEAN
(TO A BAROQUE COMPOSER)

Transmuting pain to poignancy
And happiness to buoyancy
Your music tones and tunes the mind,
At once enlivened and refined.

TO MOZART

Your music is a flower
Of summer's final hour.

TO A HAWAIIAN HULA DANCER

Your face, your being, warms with radiance
    When you dance hula: such grace and self-control!
Not only does it please your audience:
    It beautifies your soul.

BUSINESS CYCLE

CITY FOG

Fog mesmerizes morning, mutes riverglare,
Mattes boatmast forest, hillside silhouette.
One commuter's headlights simulate
Twin gray suns, lightening the air.
Across transition's bridge commuters flock
Through levitating fog, to steady clock.

OFFICE WORKER'S REVERIE—
MONDAY, 9:10 A.M.

I cannot Tab to Saturday
  Nor press Escape to weekend fun.
For pay and honor I must stay
  To finish work I have begun.

This morning, though, my blood grows gray;
  My mood is mauve; my will turns beige.
I cannot Tab to Saturday;
  The weekend seems a distant age.

This ceiling stretches half a block,
  The task before me half a day,
But I must work, ignore the clock.
  I cannot Tab to Saturday.

EUPHEMISM?

"Release," "dismiss," or "terminate," it all
Implies "You're fired." I detest the task
Of firing, but better face than mask
The chore, let candor cut than hedge or stall.

But, Lord, it could be me, and has been. Tact
Can complement with love the brutal phrase,
Good wishes modify disdain the deed conveys.
But I fired her. She was "terminated," "sacked,"
"Released," "dismissed," "let go." Rephrase? Still fact.

OFFICE

Outside the wall-high window, traffic glides
And trees breathe sunlight over lawn-trimmed street.
Inside, phones fret and signal, glades
Of paper smother desks, and we compete

With dozens like us, sweating through the town
To manufacture sales, to serve and please,
To offer something better, turn
Strangers into customers...and then, we ease

Into the evening, horizon gold
Like waterquiet after eight-oared shells
Have stroked and strained. We hum to dinner, home,
Massage of parkstroll, place where no-one sells.

GOOD HAPPENS

We buy them bottled water, sometimes juice,
Rewarding them or spurring on a sale.
I urge but not harangue them to produce,
And I stay friendly even when they fail.

I water all our greenery and clean
Each station like it was a fingernail:
Each stapler, pen cup, desk top, phone, and screen.
They know I cherish, polish each detail.

I simply do my job; I pay my rent;
A solid office manager who gets results.
Effectiveness is not a world event,
Nor am I one a billionaire consults.

Give them, our office sales team, credit. They—
Jim, Sandra, Kathy, Nick, a dozen more—
Develop leads, earn trust, and work their way
To please, not plead or pressure just to score.

They aim for excellence, not some mere stat.
I help them strive, indeed accomplish, that.

AMBITION

AMBITION

I've been traduced. I strive but not mistreat.
 I visualize my mission
 And seek the right position
To make it real. Without abuse, deceit,

Or vanity, my high-rise confidence
 Compels me to achieve, climb
 Sheer eighty-story dreams. I'm
Inspired, energized not tense.

I welcome competition:
 Do better. I congratulate
 The victor. Strive, originate,
Accomplish. Ambition—

Atomic, cosmic, or mundane—builds and cures
As medicines, museums, books, and stores.

HER CRITIC

And wars….Ambition, recognize your need
To curb your powerlust and greed.
First conquer cruelty; then we'll trust
Your claim you've been traduced.

HER CRITICAL SUPPORTER

Ambition, keep your focus and achieve!
 But, on occasion, in your tower,
 Gaze upon a simple flower,
And reflect…on something you don't quite perceive.

WEEKEND

Leisure-cushion, poultice absorbing
Stress, diffusing urge for storming
Any moment. Snooze....Stroll....Relax....
Converse, sipping wine, nibbling snacks.
Consider God, and study text.
Consider life, and relish sex.
Absorb an opal dusk or dawning...
For some cloudy, workday, alarm clock morning.

TO SEATTLE'S GULLS

Graygreen gusts chill waves
Blooming foam on pebbly city beach. Gulls
Guard balance windhovering steadiness
Above an anxious worker's lunchtime.
The gulls rode ferrywinds summermiles, snatching
Delighted tourists' French fries
In a centerfield of joy!
They stay, delighting
Winter's rare, windcold worker,
Consoled by their waterfront antics,
Cries, and freedom.

Urban wildlife! Civilization needs you!

METAMORPHOSIS

The last leaves wiggle in November breeze
As branches clutch and claw and freeze.
When all the leaves have vanished, though, the buds
Emerge, and hold
Through snowy cold
The blossoms that will redden woods
And flower branches, sky, and trees.

WEEK, SEASON, YEAR

Last weekend, a gale railed
Against the city, but failed
To budge a bowl-deep nest
Branched above a boulevard. West
Of curb, it bobs in breezes,
Endures through freezes,
As traffic stops and starts below.

First buds emerged a week ago.

TREE RING

The nighttime air is cool, and warms the mind.
The blossoms fountain trees that ring the square,
And irrigate with scent the city air.
Refreshed by springtime's vital beauty, I
Release my sorrow to the star-spread sky,
At once prepared for pain, yet unresigned.

TRUE COMMUNITY

Not common enemies, but common goals
   Create the true community.
Sincerity before mere social roles
   Breeds trust and lasting unity.

Go, search and challenge all; dare
   Grasp, grip the fabric of a proof,
And pull at every strand; pull; tear
   Until you understand its truth

Or falsity; and can determine fake
   From real. Then tell us of your test.
And note: dispute would never put at stake
   Our love. Honesty is best.

NIGHT VISION

Dusk's saffron-gold suffusions spread
To late maroon-magenta-red,
And black absorbing blue, the night.

Night deepens to transparency
And blackens into mystery:
The bottom of its pool yields light

Of origin, and poetry,
Like starlight, just inkling all we see.

*   *   *

David D. Horowitz earned bachelor's degrees in philosophy and English from the University of Washington and a master's degree in English from Vanderbilt University. He has previously published two books of poetry, *Something New and Daily* (Urban Hiker, 1981) and *Poems of a Rational Man* (Lyceum, 1989), and a book of eclectic prose, *Strength & Sympathy: Essays & Epigrams* (Rose Alley, 1996). He has published numerous poems and essays in publications as diverse as *The Lyric* and *The Sporting News*. He has taught English at Vanderbilt, Seattle Central Community College, and Shoreline Community College. For the past several years, he has worked as an office manager at a Seattle-area mortgage company. He lives in Seattle and is president of Rose Alley Press.

Photograph: Images by Edy

Other Rose Alley Press titles: